Managing C

About the series

Fast Track is a series of short, practical guides designed to get you up to speed on key business and management skills.

Written by experts with many years' experience in the field, each guide gives you instant access to key tips, advice and guidance – information you can put to work straightaway.

About the Series Editor
Andrew Forrest is a learning consultant with over 30 years' experience working with and developing people.

Managing Conflict

Anne Fox

First published in 2002
Spiro Press
Robert Hyde House
48 Bryanston Square
London W1H 2EA
Telephone: +44 (0)20 7479 2000

© Spiro Press 2002

ISBN 1 90429 812 5

British Library Cataloguing-in-Publication Data.
A catalogue record for this book is available from the
British Library.

Advice in this book is intended as guidance only. Legislation is subject to change.

Anne Fox asserts her moral right to be identified as the author of this work.

Printed by: Cromwell Press
Cover image by: Digital Vision
Cover design by: Sign Design

Acknowledgements

I would like to acknowledge the help and support I have received from my husband, Guy, who will be glad this is finally done; also Jean, George, Jane, Liz, Andrew, Michael, Mags, Lisa and Fraser who contributed unknowingly over the years. Also, friends and colleagues who encouraged me, particularly Angela Ishmael who contributed the piece on discrimination, harassment and bullying in chapter 2. Also Bob Dixon, Chrissie Wright, Julie Amber and Patricia Adams.

Contents

Introduction

Dictionary definition of conflict: verb – to dash together, to clash, to be at odds with, to be inconsistent with, to differ. Noun – a violent clashing, a trial of strength, strong disagreement.
Thesaurus: fight, battle, struggle, dispute, controversy, squabble.

Conflict in the workplace can take a number of different forms (and have different levels of seriousness) – from muted disagreement through raised voices, sometimes even violence. It can occur between team members or between managers and staff; it can also involve, directly and indirectly, external contacts, clients and suppliers. It can damage personal and business relationships. It can result from personal interaction or organisational culture. It can arise spontaneously or build over time. Whatever its form or vehemence, however, conflict can have serious consequences for individuals and organisations alike – it needs to be handled with sensitivity and authority; it cannot be ignored!

This book is intended primarily as a guide for managers, supervisors and team leaders, but will also offer invaluable advice if you are a team member. It will offer common sense responses to a range of conflict situations in the workplace, focusing on dealing with conflict in day-to-day situations rather than on how to progress conflict issues through discipline or grievance procedures. There will be some theory but the emphasis will be on the practical actions you can take as a manager to handle conflict constructively – and, as far as possible, prevent it happening in the first place. It will consider the behavioural basis of conflict and how *you*, as a manager, can influence a change in that behaviour.

Conflict is a complex area and you will sometimes need to refer issues on to your HR department or a more experienced manager; this book will highlight when.

The following diagram offers a way of looking at conflict as phases or stages we are likely to be in or travel through.

Between the two extremes of 'harmony' and 'war' lie many stepping stones to conflict. Although there are only four major areas highlighted here, in the workplace, as in any other environment, you will find many subtle stages in between.

- **'Harmony'** is the stage where a team has developed to its highest level. This team is happy and successful. Conflict is dealt with positively. In this book we will look at team development and the part that conflict and its resolution plays in reaching this 'harmony' stage.

- **'Unhappiness'** is the stage where the team's motivation level is beginning to dip. There is a feeling of unease; things just aren't right. Problems and difficulties are being suffered rather than resolved. Individuals are not able, for whatever reason, to voice their concerns. There may be an overwhelming reluctance to 'rock the boat'. Individuals may begin to change their behaviour patterns. A manager is on the spot and should be able to recognise when individuals are beginning to react differently towards each other; the odd snide remark, the look that passes between people; the atmosphere in the workplace and any downturn in productivity of the team. Managers can nip a lot of potential conflict in the bud at this stage – good communication and leadership are key.

- **'Conflict'** is the stage when issues need to be addressed. Whether it is a team or an individual in conflict, this is the point at which something needs to be done; the situation cannot be ignored. This book will take you through the key processes, highlighting when it should become an issue for HR.

- **'War'** could be regarded as the breakdown of all discipline. It could be the point where, in extreme cases, individuals have resorted to violence, or where the team 'strikes'. If you, as a manager, supervisor or team leader, have reached this stage, then YOU HAVE FAILED. This book has been written to prevent you ever reaching this stage!

Whether you are a team leader or team member, you have a responsibility to the organisation to give of your best. If you are a manager, supervisor or team leader, you have the added responsibility of managing others in the best possible environment; that means an environment with minimum conflict. When it comes to conflict, you not only have to handle issues as they arise, you also have to maintain positive relationships afterwards – after all, everyone has to meet targets, achieve results and work together day to day.

Knowing how to handle conflict effectively, therefore, is a key skill. Mastering this skill may seem daunting at first, but the effort is well worthwhile, both for yourself and for those around you.

One final, perhaps contentious, point; I would like to suggest that conflict isn't all bad! Conflict can encourage creativity and inspire new ideas; it can prevent apathy and stagnation. Without conflict, life would be very bland and uninteresting.

Conflict in the workplace

This chapter considers:
> Attitudes to conflict.

"Peace is easily maintained; trouble is easily overcome before it starts.

Deal with it before it happens.

Set things in order before there is confusion".

*From Tao Te Ching, **Lao-Tzu** (6th century BC Chinese philosopher)*

Conflict in the workplace can be as simple as a disagreement about whether to use pink paper instead of white for team communication. It can be as complex as a stand-up fight between two team members over an issue which is not work related but takes place in work time. If you are a manager, supervisor or team leader you will have to deal with the incident – and its aftermath – no matter how simple or complex.

Managers, team leaders and staff do not, in general, work in isolation. There are all sorts of rules and regulations we all adhere to. All organisations have agreed ways of doing things; some are formally written down, eg in staff handbooks or 'quality' documents such as Investors In People, others are unwritten.

When we join a new team, therefore, we are usually drawn into an established set of ground rules. We quickly find out 'how things are done around here'. We tacitly agree to a code of behaviour.

Part of this agreed code of behaviour will involve conflict resolution. How team members feel as individuals about conflict will, of course, influence how the team in general responds. Some team members will enjoy the prospect of a disagreement and argument; others will run a mile!

How you react, personally, to conflict will influence how you deal with it in a team environment. If you expect every conflict situation to be difficult, then it will be. If, on the other hand, you regard conflict as a challenge, or a problem to be wrestled with and solved, then life will be a little easier. As a manager, having a positive attitude towards conflict is vital.

As a manager you have a responsibility to deal with conflict situations involving both yourself and your team. A simple conflict situation, if not dealt with effectively, could in extreme circumstances result in violent confrontation.

If conflict frightens you, then you need to start thinking of strategies you can implement should the occasion arise. Better still, you need to know how to minimise or avoid conflict happening in the first place – though more of this later.

Let's throw you in at the deep end. Consider the following situation – how would you respond?

Exercise

You are the manager of a team of shift workers in a factory. It is 2.30pm and from your office you hear shouting. You go to investigate. Two members of your team are having a stand-up row in the middle of the shopfloor; a small crowd has gathered, it looks like it might turn nasty. What do you do? Tick your preferred option.

☐   *Go in and shout "What the hell's going on here – I want some answers, now!"*

☐   *Throw a bucket of cold water over them.*

☐   *Leave them to it.*

Which option did you tick? Did you in fact tick an option? If you didn't, well done! As you will discover, none of these responses is particularly appropriate, or effective. So how should you respond? Better still, how could you avoid such conflict happening in the first place?

Avoiding conflict

What could you have done to prevent such a situation developing? Some would say – nothing. However, burying your head in the sand and saying that it's nothing to do with you is not acceptable. If you are the manager, you have a responsibility to create an environment which enables team members to give of their best. This process starts as soon as you come into contact with your team and is reinforced each time you speak to them. If your preferred way of dealing with conflict is to ignore it, then you are contributing to the problem not resolving it. The following chapter considers some possible background causes or 'triggers' of conflict. This will help you to understand, and minimise, conflict.

Summary checklist

- ✓ Adopt a positive attitude towards conflict.
- ✓ Think about appropriate responses to conflict.
- ✓ Don't ignore the situation.

2

Possible causes of conflict

This chapter considers:
> Possible causes of conflict – both long term
and spontaneous.

Having witnessed a conflict situation between team members, where do you begin to look for possible causes? How can you become aware of the triggers which may have contributed? Below is a list of common possible causes of conflict. Some of these causes, such as 'specific problem or issue', can arise spontaneously while others, such as 'polarisation', are indicative of longer-term problems.

Possible causes of conflict

1 A specific problem or issue

2 Personal antagonism

3 Defensiveness

4 Expansion of issues

5 Poor communication

6 A 'closed' culture

7 Stress

8 Escalating mistrust

9 Polarisation

10 Discrimination, harassment and bullying.

1 A specific problem or issue

This will be short and simple, if you're lucky! The trigger for the situation might just be a spontaneous reaction to a set of circumstances or a specific comment. At its simplest, someone has perhaps misheard something and reacted; it is a misunderstanding. It arises out of a conversation, a meeting, a telephone call or a look that passes between individuals.

At its more complex, it could arise from an individual's stand on a particular issue being at odds with someone else's. It could be a difference in how a problem is tackled; indeed, whether there is a problem at all. It could arise from an individual's beliefs and values about a specific issue. It could be long standing and entrenched.

Whatever the situation, it is important to recognise that people's responses to conflict will be different. As a team member you are part of a close knit group and may know exactly how someone will react – indeed, you may be deliberately 'winding them up' to achieve a particular response. As a manager, however, you may not be so close to the team and may not know – *at that particular moment* – whether the problem is simple or complex; nonetheless you *do* need to decide quickly how to deal with the situation. Can you take the individuals aside and 'have a quick word' in an attempt to defuse the conflict informally? Alternatively, could you suggest that the individuals concerned go and have a coffee break to cool down?

2 Personal antagonism

- Charges are made – eg "You never…"; "You failed", etc.
- The other person is seen as the problem – "You always say that!"
- Labelling – "You're lazy/late", etc.

There may be personality clashes or personal antagonisms within your team of which you are unaware. There may also be a history of conflict within your team. You may become involved in a long-standing dispute which has nothing to do with the trigger for the immediate situation you find yourself in. Individuals may be using this opportunity to have a slanging match. If the conflict is between team members of equal standing that is one thing; the comments that pass between them will probably be forgotten in a short time. However, if the conflict is between the team leader or manager and a team member, then that is quite a different matter. The slanging match is then about the power balance between the two. Comments made in this situation are seldom forgotten, particularly if they have been overheard by others.

If you are the manager, supervisor or team leader, it is vital that you keep calm, however much antagonism is flying around. Don't do or say anything rash. As already mentioned, it's unlikely that you'll be alone in witnessing the situation. The rest of the team will be watching your every move. How you deal with the situation is a reflection of you as a manager, leader and/or co-worker. If you have developed a good relationship with the team up to this point, you may throw it all away in the heat of the moment with an ill-considered comment or remark. It will take a long time to recover your reputation; people have long memories when it comes to confrontation.

3 Defensiveness

- Push and push back – the 'tit for tat' reaction.
- Behaviour breeds behaviour – 'giving as good as you get'.

Conflict causes people to be defensive. They will protect whatever is important to them. Usually, people don't like to feel that someone else is 'getting one over' on them. In conflict situations where the individuals concerned know one another, they tend to mirror each other's behaviour. They have the urge to 'give as good as they get'. However, this will *not* help in resolving conflict, in finding a solution. In fact, it will probably prolong it. Such situations tend to become circular arguments. The trick, therefore, is to cut to the heart of the issue as quickly as possible. By asking in a direct, non-threatening way "What is it we disagree about?" rather than reacting defensively to what is being said, individuals may resolve the situation sooner.

4 Expansion of issues

- Issues added to other issues – everything comes out at the same time.
- More problems arise – "…and another thing!"
- Talk is less specific.

Sometimes an individual will use a conflict situation to clear the air about a number of unrelated issues, simply because they have an audience. What is more, they may not only expand the issues, they may also expand the number of participants in conflict, drawing people in, asking them to take sides. It is vital, therefore, that you remove anyone directly involved in conflict to a quiet, private area, away from prying eyes and ears, as soon as possible. Don't ask for an explanation of what's going on until you can talk to those involved privately.

People often expand the argument to other issues when they are unsure of their present argument. It is almost as though they are trying to justify their feeling of injustice and outrage. If they are having trouble 'thinking on their feet' during an argument, they may well use this tactic.

You, as the manager, may want to make a mental note of these issues, but remember that you need to deal with the *primary* issue. Subsequent issues can be dealt with at a later date.

5 Poor communication

To an extent, all conflict is the result of poor communication. Effective communication is vital, but it does take time. We all feel compelled to do more with less, and this can squeeze the amount of time we devote to planning *how* to get a message across. Yet such planning is crucial; conflict arises when people feel threatened, when things are not clear.

Another principal cause of conflict is a *breakdown* of communication. By keeping your team informed of the organisation's priorities, progress and policies (among other things) you can create a more open culture, where information moves freely around the organisation. In organisations where a team briefing system is in place, the 'message' is easily relayed to the team. Regular team briefings and team meetings can help to dispel rumours and suppress the grapevine. The manager who talks openly and honestly to their team is more in control of information than the manager who stays quiet. Remember, it is 'information' you are controlling, not the team!

Ineffective communication could be symptomatic of deeper problems that exist within the team. Most conflict results from misunderstandings. If there has been little constructive communication between team members in the past, then this may well be why conflict flares up. If teams aren't meeting on a regular basis to discuss their working practices and relationships, there could be a build up of unresolved conflict.

As the workplace has become more technology based, *methods of communication* have changed. Where we used to talk face to face with colleagues we are now more likely to send an e-mail. E-mails are fast and efficient, but one difficulty is that we tend to react to them more spontaneously than we would an old-fashioned memo, and certainly differently to how we would deal with an issue face to face. Be careful, a misplaced or flippant remark can cause offence and provoke conflict; it is good practice never to put anything in an e-mail that you wouldn't be prepared to put in a letter. Be equally scrupulous about who you include when copying people in on correspondence. Copying in is incredibly easy with e-mail, but injudicious 'ccing' can cause resentment and anger.

6 A 'closed' culture

A closed, restrictive culture can be a huge cause of conflict.

'Command and control' cultures can give rise to higher levels of conflict than more open cultures. People often feel threatened when they have little or no control over their individual workload and situation; communication breakdowns are likely. If you are a manager it is in your interests to give your team a measure of control over their work methods and environment. In a restrictive or closed culture some individuals will actively look for mischief as a way of gaining more control over their work. When you impose yet further restrictions and constraints on the individual there will be conflict – whether it is obvious to those around or not. Think of disputes where work teams resort to a 'work to rule'. Where before they did what needed to be done, they now only do as they are instructed. On the surface, they are 'only doing their job' but the effect of this is conflict.

In contrast, the empowered team will develop ways of dealing internally with conflict. Conflict reveals itself more quickly and is dealt with in a much more positive, constructive and open manner. This is much healthier; the environment contributes to a more productive team.

Whether you work in a 'command and control' or an 'empowered' culture, conflict is going to happen. What will differ is the way in which it is resolved.

7 Stress

First, we need to distinguish between 'pressure' and 'stress'. A certain amount of pressure can inspire and improve performance, but too much and it becomes 'stress', with negative effects on our work and health. Conflict and stress go hand in hand. Conflict happens because there is a difference in how people see a given situation. Stress happens when there is a perceived difference in our ability to cope with the demands made upon us.

Pressures at work that provoke stress and conflict

- **The workplace** – the working environment and physical conditions (space, privacy, noise levels, etc).
- **The job** – the actual job itself (workload, involvement in decisions, etc).
- **Travelling** – commuting, traffic, assignments away from home, etc.
- **Roles** – responsibilities, boundaries.
- **Career** – ambitions and expectations of success.
- **Relationships** – both working and personal.
- **Individual** – standards we set ourselves, ability to cope with change, suitability for the job, etc.
- **Work-life balance** – more usually the 'imbalance'!

What can you do to reduce stress in the workplace, and so reduce possible conflict flash-points? Some of the strategies discussed in later chapters will help. As a manager or team leader, you are on the spot. You can alleviate stress but, remember, you can also contribute to the team's stress levels, albeit unwittingly.

As already mentioned, communication and leadership are key skills for any manager. Your strength or weakness in these areas will influence stress levels. Unclear decisions, changing priorities, insufficient information, unreasonable demands or expectations made on the team will all result in increased stress. You may think that running around dealing with everything yourself shows that you are busy but the team may perceive your behaviour as only adding to their problems.

Remember *stress is the difference between the demands made upon us and our perceived ability to cope.*

8 Escalating mistrust

• Becoming more and more entrenched.

The longer a conflict goes on the more complex it becomes. Even usually rational adults begin to doubt what is being said. We don't have the ability to recall everything we say verbatim, so the longer a conflict situation goes on the more difficult it is to remember exactly what has been said. Self-doubt starts to creep in. As emotional beings, we start to question the other person's motives for the conflict. We look for justification – why is he/she saying that? When did I say that to them? What are they thinking? What are they *not* saying? Issues are filed away ready to throw out the next time there is an argument.

Regular team meetings can provide all team members with an opportunity to ask for clarification and air their concerns.

9 Polarisation

• **Seeking allies** – gaining support from others.
• **Groups organised into two camps** – 'If you're not with me then you're against me!'
• **No backing down** – people dig their heels in.
• **Nothing can ever be the same again** – people have long memories.
• **'Fight to the death'** – the conflict becomes a battle of wills.

If your team is in the early stages of its development then the group may well fragment into camps. There is a natural tendency to look for support amongst colleagues. Again, this is a symptom of a power struggle. The more people we can draw into our camp the stronger our position will appear to be. After all, if all these people agree with us then there must be a problem!

Team leaders, and indeed team members, must deal with the *issues* not the personalities. You cannot allow yourself to be drawn into different camps. By standing back and assessing the situation before deciding on any action you will be seen to be fairer in the long run.

10 Discrimination, harassment and bullying

Conflict situations which arise out of behaviours based in discrimination, harassment or bullying need to be handled carefully. It is a complex, problematic area and it is important to involve the HR department, or a senior manager, if you suspect these behaviours are going on in your organisation. These issues are only touched on briefly below in a piece by Angela Ishmael, author of the excellent *Harassment, Bullying and Violence at Work*. Angela's piece will help you define and recognise these behaviours; it also offers some basic advice if you are the target of such behaviours.

Make sure all members of staff understand what constitutes discrimination, harassment and bullying.

Discrimination

Discrimination occurs when someone is treated less favourably on grounds of their difference or because of a characteristic; mainly sex, gender, marital status, disability, colour, race, nationality or ethnic origin.

Discrimination is about people's actions and the effects of their actions, not their thought processes, intentions, opinions or beliefs. Discrimination is not the same as prejudice or 'isms'.

- Prejudice literally means 'pre-judging' someone; knowing next to nothing about them but jumping to conclusions because of some characteristic, such as their appearance.
- Racism is the belief that some races are superior to others, based on the false idea that different physical characteristics (like skin colour) or ethnic background make some people better than others.
- Sexism is the belief that one gender is superior to another (normally male superiority vs female inferiority).
- In legal terms (in the UK) you do not have to prove that someone intended to discriminate against you: as with harassment and bullying, it is sufficient only to show that the outcome of their action was that you received less favourable treatment.

Prejudice and power are the roots from which discrimination springs, and when discrimination is enacted harassment and bullying occur.

Harassment and bullying
- Harassment and bullying is discriminatory behaviour that is unwelcome, unreciprocated and unwanted.
- It can take the form of physical, verbal or non-verbal conduct.
- It is behaviour that is determined by its impact on the person on the receiving end, even if no harm was intended.
- The target of the behaviour determines what is unacceptable, within given boundaries.

Harassment, a form of direct discrimination, can occur on the following grounds:
- Sex
- Race
- Disability

- Heterosexist (against lesbians and gay men)
- Religion (often known as sectarianism in Northern Ireland).

Bullying is also a form of harassment, however, it differs in that it can occur generally and is not always directed at an individual because of one of the grounds mentioned above. It is not unusual, however, for someone to use, for example, bullying tactics to abuse a disabled person. There is more of an element of intention to harm with bullying; bullies often know that their targets will suffer negative effects from their behaviours (even if, sometimes, they don't know how to behave otherwise).

Harassment and bullying are dangerous and devastating; they can rob people of their self-worth and cause untold stress. It is often difficult to get others to take harassment and bullying seriously, because what may be unacceptable behaviour to you may be totally acceptable to someone else. However, it is vital that complaints of harassment and bullying are taken seriously, even if on the surface the behaviour does not appear to be a problem.

You need to be able to recognise harassment and bullying, whether it is happening to yourself or a member of your team.

How do you recognise harassment and bullying?

The obvious behaviours are the easiest to spot – unnecessary patting and touching, shouting and swearing, name calling, embarrassing people in front of others, sexual innuendo and racial slurs, pin-up calendars and rude or aggressive e-mails ('flame mail').

The hidden, less obvious, types of behaviour are the most difficult to deal with and, unfortunately, happen more frequently. Experiencing excess criticism, having your goals changed and making it difficult to meet them, gossiping and back-biting, and others taking credit for your efforts (yet never the blame when things go wrong) all have the effect of making you doubt yourself and wonder whether you are really suffering harassment and bullying.

This is why identifying and labelling the behaviour is important because it makes clear sense of what you are experiencing.

If you are a manager who has a team member/s experiencing these negative behaviours, you need to seek support from your HR department or a senior manager immediately. Perhaps, however, you yourself are experiencing these behaviours directly? If so, whether you are a team leader or team member, and whether you have the support of HR or not, you will also need to handle these behaviours on a personal level. The question is, how?

Handling discrimination, harassment and bullying

- To challenge harassment, bullying and all forms of discrimination you have to be courageous and take control. Getting in touch with your personal power and taking responsibility by thinking positively and boosting your self-worth is essential. You need to ask yourself "What are the consequences for me (and others) if I decide to do nothing?"

- Talk to someone you can trust – never suffer in silence. Being afraid to talk about your experience only serves to make it worse and the perception that it is almost impossible to deal with may grow. Take time out with those that will support you to plan a strategy that will help you stop the harassment and bullying.

- Keep a journal or diary of events. This can help in two ways: first, keeping a log of the perpetrator's behaviour, right down to every little detail, may be vital evidence if you have to deal with your situation on a more formal basis. Secondly, writing down your thoughts and feelings about your situation can help to clarify it and ease some of the pain you may be experiencing.

- Only if appropriate, challenge the harasser or bully face to face, and in an assertive manner. Sometimes, simply telling the individual to stop can be enough (some people are unaware of the negative effects of their behaviour and challenging them may make them more aware and cautious in the future).

- If your organisation has procedures for dealing with harassment and bullying, use them if necessary. If you are a team member, approach your line manager, who in turn should approach HR to set procedures in motion. If your organisation does not have formal procedures or support mechanisms to deal with these behaviours, seek external advice from a public advice centre, solicitor, law centre, union representative, etc.

The culture of the organisation and/or industry you work in may suggest that racism and sexism is 'just the way it is around here…' That doesn't mean to say it is acceptable! As a manager, supervisor or team leader you are in the ideal position to influence a change in current thinking. Don't feel that you have to change the world, start with your team.

Most conflict situations occur between two individuals but, as already stated, people do not usually work in isolation. The ripples caused by arguments and disagreements will have a knock-on effect on the whole team. In the next chapter, we explore the key stages of team development and identify potential conflict flash-points.

Summary checklist

✓ Be aware of, and understand, possible causes of conflict.

✓ Remove the individuals involved in conflict to a quiet, private area as soon as possible.

✓ Poor communication is at the root of most conflict – communicate regularly and consistently with your team.

3

Conflict during team development

This chapter considers:
> Key stages in team development.
> Conflict flash-points.

You may be familiar with the idea that teams go through an evolutionary process, namely *forming*, *storming*, *norming* and *performing*. This is not dissimilar to the diagram in the Introduction showing harmony, unhappiness, conflict and war. This process has many interesting angles to it; including a conflict dynamic. Conflict is an inevitable, and vital, part of team development.

Stages in team development

Forming

This is the stage when the team first gets together. In the beginning of team development people are exploring each other's behaviour. There will be lots of boundary testing – how far can we go? Serious conflict tends not to figure too highly at this stage. Individuals usually keep their emotions in check for fear of overstepping a boundary which is as yet undefined. People tend to be well behaved, at least on the surface. Only when team members begin to get to know each other better and move on to the next stage of development will conflict situations become more obvious.

Storming

This is the most difficult stage in team development, and the one where conflict is most apparent. Because the team members are becoming more familiar with one other, it is easier to express disagreement. Power and the internal workings of the team become an issue. Individuals are 'flexing their muscles' within the group. They may try to impress the other team members (especially the manager) by showing what they know, who they know and how they got to where they are in the company. With all of that going on, there is increased potential for conflict.

With familiarity comes questioning: "Why are we doing it this way?" "I want to do it my way!" Individuals begin to defend their own beliefs and gather like-minded people to themselves. In conflict terms, this means that when there is disagreement the team may well fragment into different camps. There is plenty of activity in this stage, some of which is productive and some not. A pecking order begins to emerge and this can also cause conflict. The stronger personalities will assert themselves, possibly at the expense of the quieter members of the team. An alert manager will recognise this and include all members of the team in discussions. This is a relatively noisy stage; there will be lots of talking (formal and informal), differences of opinion and arguments.

Norming

The team begins to settle down. In conflict terms, this is the stage when the team will try to avoid conflict in an effort to achieve and maintain harmony. Maintaining the *status quo* is vital. The team's ground rules have been established and there is plenty of evidence of friendliness, team cohesion and confiding in one other. The team will be discovering each other's strengths and weaknesses. As the team members mature in their dealings with one another conflict moves into a different phase. Where before, in the storming phase, conflict was difficult, in the norming phase conflict becomes a more positive action. Team members will actively work issues out. Conflict is not seen as a threat but as an opportunity to explore new ways of looking at problems.

Performing

The team achieves much of what it decides to implement. Individuals understand and, more importantly, accept how others think and feel about contentious issues and will work positively to resolve situations. At this stage, team members will seek to make things work. They are constructive in their decision making and implementation of change and, as a result, conflict levels are low. This stage is the 'harmony' referred to in the diagram in the Introduction. The team is happy, successful and conflict is dealt with positively.

Mourning

There is an additional stage in team development that is sometimes forgotten or neglected and that is **mourning.** When a team disbands, or a new member joins an established team, the dynamics can be upset for a short time. This can become a conflict flash-point. The team may be unhappy about being disbanded or reconfigured and will still feel loyalty to the original team. During this time there will be many references to how things were done in the past. There will be fondness expressed for the 'old' team. The manager who ignores this emotional time may well have a problem. It would be worthwhile having a celebration of some sort at this time. Such a celebration would not only recognise the achievements of the 'old' team but would also offer an opportunity for the 'new' team to socialise.

Summary of possible conflict triggers during team development

Forming stage	individuals with different agendas
	unclear objectives
	unstable structure
Storming stage	lack of trust
	not enough time spent discussing problems
	individuals jostling for position
	time of high emotion
	team roles still unsure
	disagreements around the 'how' of the job
Norming stage	inflexibility
	lack of creativity
	'that's not how it's done around here' attitude
	over-identification of team as single entity
	reluctance in accepting new member
	inward-looking focus
Performing stage	perceptions of external groups
	'resting on laurels' syndrome
Mourning stage	over-indulgence
	reluctance to leave the past behind and move on
	fear of change.

As the manager of a team you have a responsibility to manage your team effectively. Not only do you need to lead the team (as a complete group), you also need to manage the individuals within the team. Not only do you need to develop your personal management style but your conflict resolution style too.

In the next chapter we consider how to recognise and understand conflict, and your reactions to it.

Summary checklist

✓ Understand the four key stages in team development – forming, storming, norming and performing – and their different implications for conflict.

What does conflict look like to you?

This chapter considers:
> How you perceive conflict.
> Recognising signs of conflict.

So what do you need to watch out for when it comes to conflict; what are the recognisable signs that a team member (or a customer or supplier for that matter) could be in conflict?

An obviously angry person could have a flushed complexion, be breathing shallowly, sweating, staring, clenching their fists, speaking quickly or be incoherent in their speech. Remember, though, that their behaviour could be out of all proportion to the actual incident and that the person who walks away could also be in conflict; they simply have a different way of expressing it. The individual that is usually chatty and smiling who suddenly becomes quiet and withdrawn could be as angry as the individual previously described, they just don't show it so obviously. Only by getting to know your team members as individuals can you recognise their responses and start to pre-empt possible conflict situations.

Exercise

This exercise will help you build a clearer picture of some of the behaviours which can contribute to a conflict situation.

In your mind, think of a person with whom you are, or have been, in conflict. Visualise this person as completely as possible.

How do they look? (Think of their dress, style, posture, gestures, face, eyes.)

What is their usual attitude towards you? (Kindly, patronising, subservient, pushy?)

What do you like about this person?

What irritates you about them?

How are you creative together?

How do you frustrate one another?

What do they say that irritates you?

What kinds of behaviour most offend you?

How do you show your annoyance?

How do you express yourself – your enthusiasm, your sympathy, your disagreement, your appreciation of this person?

Is there an organisational cost to this conflict situation?

What would you most like to say to this person?

How might you say it?

Are you only in conflict about how to do something, not whether it should be done?

Behaviour breeds behaviour. Do you always react in the same way to a particular individual? Does that encourage thoughts of conflict? Are you in conflict with someone because you suspect they don't like you or because you think they are unfairly favoured in some way? Perhaps you just don't like how they dress or speak?

If you have a preconceived notion of how conflict looks, sounds and feels like then you may 'talk yourself into' a situation. If you expect there to be conflict then that is what will happen – it's a self-fulfilling prophecy. If your internal self-talk is telling you that you always have a problem with this person/situation then your body language and tone (which accounts for 93% of someone's impression of you) may well be sending that message even before you say a word! Management is not a popularity contest. It would be great if everyone liked everyone else but this is not the way of the world. As a manager, you will have to make unpopular decisions or ask individuals to do tasks that they may not enjoy – that's the job. If you complicate it further by making assumptions about how team members *might* behave, life will become unbearable.

Try not to pigeonhole your team members. Deal with conflict situations as impartially as you can. Put your assumptions and preconceived ideas to one side and deal with conflict as you find it. You will be doing your team a disservice if you bring a load of unnecessary baggage to your role and management style. Put yourself in their position – how would you like to be managed by someone who assumes that because you dress, speak or act in a particular way you are therefore a troublemaker?

Our assumptions can become part of our culture; the way we interpret the world. The continued use of certain phrases in our language can help perpetuate ways of looking at the world.

Traditional views of conflict

The English language is full of rich, colourful phrases and proverbs; some of these reflect views, myths and strategies for resolving conflict. These phrases are handed down over time and indicate 'traditional' wisdom.

Exercise

Look at the phrases below. How typical are they of your attitude towards conflict? Tick either 'Very typical', 'Fairly typical' or 'Not at all typical'.

		Very typical	Fairly typical	Not at all typical
1	*It is easier to refrain, than to retreat, from a quarrel.*	☐	☐	☐
2	*Soft words win hard hearts.*	☐	☐	☐
3	*You scratch my back, I'll scratch yours.*	☐	☐	☐
4	*Might overcomes right.*	☐	☐	☐
5	*Truth lies in knowledge, not in majority opinion.*	☐	☐	☐
6	*He who fights and runs away lives to fight another day.*	☐	☐	☐
7	*No person has the final answer but each has a piece to contribute.*	☐	☐	☐

8	Stay away from people who disagree with you.	☐	☐	☐
9	Victory is won by people who believe in winning.	☐	☐	☐
10	'Tit for tat' is fair play.	☐	☐	☐
11	Only the person who is willing to give up their monopoly on truth can ever profit from the truths that others hold.	☐	☐	☐
12	Avoid quarrelsome people as they will only make your life miserable.	☐	☐	☐
13	Bring your conflicts into the open and face them directly; only then will the best solution be discovered.	☐	☐	☐
14	Put your foot down where you mean to stand.	☐	☐	☐
15	Frankness, honesty and trust will move mountains.	☐	☐	☐
16	There is nothing so important you have to fight for it.	☐	☐	☐
17	When both people give in half way, a fair settlement is achieved.	☐	☐	☐
18	Nothing lowers the level of the conversation more than raising your voice.	☐	☐	☐

This exercise will give you an indication of how you regard conflict. Look back at your responses – do you seem to address conflict openly and directly or do you try and ignore it? Do you believe in 'winning' conflict at all costs?

'Traditional' wisdom is handed down from parents, school, even senior managers. Such wisdom may sound as though it is the truth but a little analysis shows that it is only *one* way of looking at the world. How many of these phrases reflect your attitude? Indeed, do you regularly use any of these phrases? If we use or hear these phrases often enough, we begin to believe them. As a result, they begin to influence our behaviour.

When you are evaluating how you dealt with a particular situation, give some thought to your attitude and the language you used. Did you actually use some of the phrases mentioned? Did they betray how you felt about an individual or situation?

If you find conflict difficult it may be because of your mindset. There are many ways to deal with conflict, the trick is to find one which works for you! In the next chapter we will look at different conflict resolution styles.

Summary checklist

✓ Learn to recognise the signs of conflict.

✓ Be aware of your attitude towards conflict, and the effect this has on your response to people and situations.

Conflict resolution styles

> This chapter considers:
> > Different conflict resolution styles – are you a turtle, shark, teddy bear, fox or owl?
> Are you a combination of styles?
> > The pros and cons of the different styles.

Different people have different conflict resolution styles. These are learned (usually in childhood) and can seem to be automatic responses. We don't even think about a strategy, we just get on with it. This is all very well, but different responses work well in some situations, badly in others. You need to have a flexible approach. The good news is that if a conflict resolution style is learned then it can be unlearned or adapted.

Your conflict resolution style is affected by:

- The importance you attach to your personal goals.
- The importance you attach to particular relationships.

Essential conflict resolution styles

We can identify five essential conflict resolution styles based on these two concerns.

The TURTLE – withdrawing into your shell.

Pro: By extricating yourself from the situation, you don't have to deal with it.
By ignoring the people with whom you are in conflict, life never gets difficult.

Con: Could be seen as cautionary; not sufficiently proactive.
It is crucial that you don't inflame an already explosive incident by ignoring it!

The SHARK – succeeds by overpowering the opposition.

Pro: Shark style has strength and purpose. This is important at the right time; when you need to get involved or elicit information.

Con: Sharks only have their own interests at heart. Their whole strategy is based on intimidation, attack and aggression. Can be perceived as bullying.

The TEDDY BEAR – relationships are all-important.

Pro: Teddy bears need to be loved and wanted by others; feelings are their primary concern.

Con: They will do anything to maintain harmony. They will try to paper over the cracks by encouraging everyone to stay friends.

The FOX – looks for the middle ground.

Pro: Is moderately concerned with their own goals and relationships with others.

They will give up part of their goals and go for compromise.

Con: Foxes often come out of their bolt holes for a short time then, having given you the run around, retreat to a place of safety.

The OWL – values highly their own goals and relationships.

Pro: They view a conflict situation as a problem to be solved and a means to an end in improving relationships. Owls allow time to consider all the options.

Con: They are not satisfied until solutions are found and tensions and negative feelings resolved. They may take too long to reach a solution.

Each of these styles is powerful in its own right – but each has something different to offer. Our tendency may be to favour one style rather than another but each has its own reward in the management of conflict.

Turtle – encourages reflection
Shark – gets information
Teddy bear – maintains relationships
Fox – looks for compromise
Owl – looks for a pragmatic solution.

So, pulling together all of these styles could provide a more rounded strategy for dealing with conflict.

Exercise

This exercise asks you to concentrate on conflict resolution style. Think of a situation where you, or someone you know, dealt with conflict well. Try to concentrate not on the detail of the conflict itself but on the person who has to deal with the situation.

1   *Which of the above styles was used?*

2   *What about the language and tone of the style? What words or phrases can you remember?*

3   *What about the non-verbal language? Were you aware of body language?*

4   *Where was the situation dealt with?*

5   *What did you, or could you, learn from the situation about the 'how' of dealing with conflict?*

Having thought through this exercise you may have noticed how useful it is to analyse actions a little more closely. By picturing the conflict resolution styles as animals it is easier to identify them. So, are you a fox or a shark? Or have you discovered that actually you are a bit of all of them? Different circumstances will call for different styles; so, too, will different people. Consider the following.

The turtle approach may be appropriate when the situation is becoming heated. If you know that you – or the person with whom you are in conflict – have a short fuse, then developing a turtle style may help you to slow down and avoid inflaming the situation. Do you have to deal with the situation immediately?

The shark approach is direct – necessary when you need information. Also, there are times when you as a manager have to be in charge. The buck stops with you. This style encourages you to be seen as a leader.

The teddy bear approach reminds you that we all like to be liked. Sometimes we get so wrapped up in the business of business that we forget that our team members are human beings with feelings and egos that need to be looked after. Using the teddy bear style is useful when it's relationships that need fixing or when a more strident style would do damage.

The fox approach allows you to stay ahead of the team. You know what you need to achieve through the team's efforts and the distance between you allows some room for compromise. Knowing what is expected of you, as the team leader, and knowing your team, and what they are capable of achieving, ensures that you can negotiate on their behalf. Only then can you manage the team effectively and with minimum conflict.

The owl approach is useful when there are a lot of options to consider. This style enables you to look at the conflict situation as a problem to be solved in a logical, rational manner. It also encourages you to look inside yourself for the wisdom that you have gained through your previous experience.

As mentioned before, team members that get to know one another through better communication have a better idea, too, of how to deal with one another in a conflict situation. Team-building exercises which encourage discussion along these lines will benefit everyone. Perhaps playing the game 'If x was a … (pet, wild animal, vegetable, car, etc) which would they be?' will allow the team to explore how they perceive one other. It will certainly prompt a lot of discussion.

By now you will have noticed that a lot of conflict resolution involves recognising how, and why, we respond to certain situations. This is the topic for the next chapter.

Summary checklist

✓ Understand the five basic conflict resolution styles – their pros and cons.

✓ Use different styles for different situations and people.

Behaviour

> This chapter discusses:
> > The power of behaviour.
> > Aggressive, manipulative, passive and assertive behaviour.
> > Resolving problems assertively.

Behaviour is defined as conduct; how we show ourselves to others. We learn most behaviours as we grow up. We watch our parents, our siblings, our school mates – indeed, anyone with whom we come into contact. We are able to assimilate unconsciously their actions into our own. The impact of other media over the years adds to our repertoire. I am not suggesting that we learn behaviours wholesale, and use them like robots; what I *am* suggesting is that we are *influenced* by watching others in all kinds of ways, some more direct than others.

In conflict situations, therefore, we will use, consciously or unconsciously, behaviour that we have witnessed in others. We will have virtually no time to 'decide' how to react but our actions could have serious consequences. An understanding of behaviour will give us an insight into ourselves and others. Whether you are a manager, supervisor, team leader or team member this insight will be useful.

The power of behaviour

We learn from an early age what we need to *do* to influence others around us. Take, for example, a child in a supermarket. I am sure we have all seen the temper tantrum thrown by a small child that wants sweets. A flustered parent – whose only desire is to get through the checkout and back to the car in one piece – can usually be seen trying to reason with the child. The child does not understand reason. They know from previous experience that if they make enough noise the adult will usually give in to their demands. The child is *rewarded* for this behaviour by getting the sweets it wanted. The adult, however, walks away feeling embarrassed and guilty.

What has this got to do with behaviour in the workplace?

The child that is rewarded for this behaviour (and never learns any other way of asking for what it wants) grows into an adult that will continue to use similar behaviour. This behaviour is *manipulative.* By manipulating the situation or the feelings of the other person the child/adult gets what they want. Remember, the key to this behaviour is making the other person feel bad enough that they give in to the demands being made. In conflict situations, this can be very difficult behaviour to deal with.

Exercise

Picture in your mind a serious conflict situation you have experienced, or think back to the scenario outlined at the beginning of chapter 1.

1   *What actions did you see in the other person?*

2   *What sort of words did they use?*

> **3** *What did you do and say?*
>
> **4** *How did you feel?*
>
> **5** *Now list the negative signs that you saw or heard, eg swearing, pushing, crying, silence, etc.*

These signs can be identified as aggressive, manipulative or passive behaviours. There is another kind of behaviour – assertive. However, if you have imagined the worst scenario, there is unlikely to be evidence of this!

If we could draw a spectrum of behaviours it might look like the following, with aggressive behaviours at one extreme and passive at the other.

Aggressive   Manipulative   Passive

So what constitutes these behaviours?

Aggressive behaviour violates the rights of others by doing some or all of the following:

- Interrupting someone while they are speaking.
- Imposing views on others.
- Making decisions for others.
- Accusing, blaming and finding fault.
- Harming or inconveniencing others rather than ourselves.
- Using power, position or status over others.

Aggressive behaviour can be frightening to those around us. It relies on the intimidation of others whether directly or indirectly. Aggressive behaviour at its worst can be violent either physically or verbally. Don't be aggressive yourself, or do something which might be perceived as aggressive behaviour; ie throwing a bucket of cold water over those in conflict!

Manipulative behaviour plays on the other person's emotions by:
* Sulking.
* Crying at will.
* Making sarcastic remarks.
* Keeping silent.

Manipulative behaviour can be cunning and devious. The whole point of using it is to get some sort of 'payback'; whether that's making the other person upset or getting them to do something.

Passive behaviour:
* Avoids confrontation.
* The person can appear as the victim.
* Tends to defer to other people.
* Body language tends to be withdrawn and inward-looking.
* Puts off decision making.

Passive behaviour is frustrating to those around us. In the workplace, we need to get things done. If we withdraw and make no contribution to the team's efforts or continually defer to others we will be perceived as not pulling our weight.

Finally, **assertive** behaviour is:
* Adult.
* Rational.
* Logical.
* Self-controlled.
* Open, honest and direct.

Assertive behaviour is based in the belief that we are adult and take responsibility for our actions. Being assertive is not about being demanding and 'standing up for our rights' in an inappropriately powerful way. It is about having the self-confidence to state our case or our opinions but *at the same time* allowing the other person the same right. It is about asking for what we want while recognising the needs of others.

Implicit in assertiveness is the concept that we each have certain rights:

- To hold and express different views.
- To be listened to.
- To be taken seriously.
- To disagree.
- To be treated with respect.

Assertiveness is about making adult choices based on these rights. It is about dealing with *issues* not personalities.

Assertiveness is the key to good, clear, professional communication. It is choosing the most appropriate response to a given situation.

So how do you begin to deal with a conflict situation in an assertive manner? The following model will help you.

Being assertive

First, you need to be clear about what you want to achieve, and what you are prepared to compromise on to achieve it.

1 'Own' the feelings that the problem raises in you. Use direct 'I' statements, this shows that you own what you say, eg "I feel unhappy when you…" Say what it is you want, or what you perceive the problem to be, eg "I want you to…" or "I think the problem is…" Be clear when you speak. Use a pleasant tone, don't raise your voice.

2 Listen to what the other person has to say and acknowledge their response. Use appropriate body language, for example nodding your head. It is important to show that you are listening. Maintain an 'open', non-threatening posture; be careful not to invade other people's personal space.

3 If you feel unable to compromise, acknowledge the other person's feelings but restate your position. You may need to change the language you use.

What you are trying to establish, using this model, is the common ground. The assertiveness model suggested can help do just that.

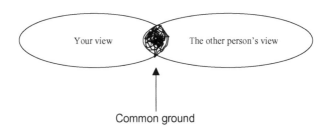

Common ground

By being logical and rational in approach you will have a clearer picture of any conflict. When we wrap conflict up in extraneous issues, we make resolution that much more difficult. We need to be prepared when we enter into assertive discussions. We can then 'choose' our response rather than reacting to what is being said during the conversation, so lessening the risk of causing yet more conflict. Aggressive behaviour is a *reaction*. We don't have time to think about the best way of dealing with the situation – so we lash out. Hopefully not as violently as shown opposite!

Assertive behaviour is a response. It is a chosen action which is adult, rational, confident and appropriate to the situation.

In conflict, then, assertiveness is a useful skill to master.

Assertiveness is a technique which encourages consistency of approach. Practise the skill and you will earn the respect of others for doing so, and it will make managing your team easier. Your team will come to know that you are not going to respond inappropriately, that you will deal with them fairly; as a result you become more approachable.

Assertiveness techniques can help manage conflict by enabling you to:

- State what you want.
- 'Own' the feelings attached to the situation.
- Clearly identify areas of agreement, disagreement and common ground.
- Support your ideas with prepared, objective evidence.
- Avoid personalising conflict.
- Be prepared to change opinion.
- Negotiate a positive response.

Resolving problems assertively

1 Use 'I' not 'you'.

2 State your feelings using language which does not inflame the situation. Think about the words you use and the effect they will have on others. How would you respond if these words were directed at you? Insults, swear words and gestures will be remembered for a very long time after the actual conflict is forgotten!

3 State the behaviour which is causing the problem.

4 Avoid criticism.

5 Listen to the other person.

6 Create empathy by acknowledging the other person's side of the conflict.

7 Negotiate in the common ground.

8 Offer possible solutions that may move the discussion forward.

9 Be prepared to compromise, but be aware of your final fall-back position.

10 State your understanding of any resolution reached.

Here is an example of this approach.

Example

Maggie: I appreciate that you have been dealing with a very complex and time-consuming case recently, however, I am concerned that you have not answered two queries which you received from customers last week. They have both spoken to me personally

> about it because whenever they telephone you are out. What is the problem?
>
> **Liz:** I couldn't answer their questions without doing a lot of research. As I've got a more pressing priority, I just put them to one side.
>
> **Maggie:** I can understand that you haven't got time to do extra research at the moment. What can we do about getting the answers for the customers?
>
> **Liz:** If the office junior has some spare time, it might be good experience for them to do the research.
>
> **Maggie:** How long do you think it will take to get the answers?
>
> **Liz:** If you or someone more experienced could give George some guidance, I should think he'd be able to answer one of the queries today.
>
> **Maggie:** OK. If you give me the details now, I will brief George and get him on to it. I'll then go back to the customers concerned and let them know what's happening – is that OK?

Contrast this with the following, aggressive, example.

Example

> **Maggie:** Damn it Liz, why can't you ever get things done? Do I have to do it all myself? I've just had an earful from customers because you can't get your act together!
>
> **Liz:** I'm doing the best I can.
>
> **Maggie:** And you think that's good enough?
>
> **Liz:** I've been really busy, I don't seem to have time to do everything.
>
> **Maggie:** If you can't do it, there are thousands out there that can. No more half-baked excuses – get it done, now!

The first example shows an appropriate, rational and adult response to a problem. It shows an encouraging and supportive style of management. The second example shows intolerance, disrespect and a poor grasp of 'people' skills. It does nothing to promote a good working environment, and won't resolve the problem.

Assertiveness works. It can defuse a potential conflict situation and promote a better working environment.

Managing conflict – the 'ladder of inference'

An alternative technique (still based on assertive behaviour) is explored by Peter Senge in his *Fifth Discipline FieldBook*.

Senge suggests that we have already built a 'ladder of inference'. When we engage in conversation we not only hear the words that others use, we are also aware of their body language (the non-verbal signals). We add our own interpretation to what we see and hear and then draw conclusions. We build a 'ladder', higher and higher, based on each subsequent conversation (see diagram opposite).

We first *observe behaviour* in others and we experience our own. Then we *pick and choose* (consciously and unconsciously) from those observations what is valuable (ie important) to us. We then *add cultural and personal meanings* based on religion, upbringing and education, in a predominately unconscious way. We now feel we can *make assumptions* based on these meanings. We can *draw conclusions* because we have built a database based on what we understand in our own world. We feel justified in *adopting beliefs* about those around us because we 'know' we are right. Finally, we *take actions* based on these beliefs.

If we never take time out to analyse what we observe, we run the risk of building our 'ladder of inference' on very shaky data. Using

TAKE ACTIONS – based on beliefs

ADOPT BELIEFS – about the world

Our beliefs affect what data we select next time.

DRAW CONCLUSIONS

MAKE ASSUMPTIONS – based on meanings

ADD MEANINGS – cultural and personal

SELECT DATA FROM OBSERVATIONS

OBSERVABLE DATA

the diagram, take a few moments to do your own step-by-step analysis of a belief you hold.

Senge has developed a technique which helps us to question our own 'ladder of inference'; this can be useful when dealing with conflict. The idea behind this is to stop the conflict conversation and take some time out to question your thinking and reasoning; and others'. You might like to try this as another strategy. Bear in mind that you need to approach this in an adult, rational manner. The language – both verbal and non-verbal – needs to be logical, non-manipulative, non-aggressive, confident and appropriate.

Senge suggests that we use the following questions to encourage discussion in a conflict situation.

What is the observable evidence behind what I've just heard?

Does everyone agree on what the evidence is?

Can you run me through your reasoning?

How did we get from that evidence to these assumptions?

When you said " [your implication]", did you mean "[my inference]"?

You will find it helpful to think of the diagram while asking these questions.

I hope this chapter has given you some useful strategies. The key to their success is practice, practice, practice. Knowing the theory is one thing, it's in the doing that we learn.

In the next chapter we look at some useful do's and don'ts.

Summary checklist

✓ Recognise and understand the power of different kinds of behaviour.

✓ Respond to conflict situations assertively.

✓ Question your own 'ladder of inference'.

7

Useful do's and don'ts

> This chapter outlines:
> > Useful do's and don'ts of managing conflict.

So what else can we consider when trying to resolve conflict situations? Here are a few guidelines, which are really just common sense.

DO

✓ **Establish ground rules for dealing with conflict as soon as possible** – organise a meeting to discuss the situation. As discussed in chapter 3, a team will fall into patterns of behaviour come what may. Your responsibility as a manager, team leader or team member is to agree strategies as much as you can between each other. Doing this in an adult, open and honest manner during a team meeting is by far the best option. By setting out some ground rules you are saying to each other that conflict will happen but that you have a way of dealing with it which will resolve the situation and maintain the team's performance.

✓ **Bring conflict out at the earliest 'safe' time** – when you feel the team is ready to deal with conflict in an adult manner. Look for the 'moment of truth', ie a moment when a solution is possible.

✓ **Remain impartial** – you need to stay 'on the fence' while you are [informally] investigating a conflict situation. It is not advisable to be part of any formal investigation if, as line manager, you have prior knowledge of the individual/s concerned.

✓ **Encourage team ownership of outcomes** – the more people that 'buy in' to the outcome the better.

✓ **Be realistic** – you need to live in the real world!

✓ **Be honest** – admit that there is a difference of opinion, approach or perception. An assertive person values honesty and a commitment to the truth. Value openness.

✓ **Resolve the difficulty to the satisfaction of both parties** – not 'I win/you lose' but 'We solved the problem together'. If any issue is left unresolved then it may come back to haunt you later. It also means that the individuals concerned go away with a feeling of not having completed the process.

✓ **Communicate** – never stop talking to your team. In regular one-to-one meetings you can often nip problems in the bud, encourage good performance and get to know individuals. Ask "How are things going?" or "What can I do to help?" At team meetings, tell the team what you are doing on their behalf. Listen to their concerns.

✓ **Encourage team activities** – team members that are comfortable with one another will air grievances early and suffer less from stress and conflict. Successful teams deal with conflict and stress more positively.

✓ **Be an ambassador for your team at a higher level** – if your team believes that you are on their side you will gain their confidence and respect.

✓ **Use a systematic approach to problem solving or managing change** – consistency engenders trust. Managers gain their team's confidence by being consistent.

✓ **Use assertiveness techniques to maintain your rights without violating other people's** – behaving as an adult, rational being shows that you are open to the needs of others.

✓ **Use conflict as a vehicle to create new ideas, gain new perspectives and improve ways of doing things** – this is often forgotten in conflict resolution. Conflict can be a positive agent for change. By bringing issues out into the open, dealing with them rationally and implementing changes, conflict will be seen as a useful tool.

✓ **Attack the problem not the person** – remember, more often than not conflict situations arise because of *how* we do something. In conflict, we need to concentrate on the issue not the personalities.

✓ **Allow the other side to let off steam** – clarify expectations and roles. Listen actively and acknowledge what is being said. Understand and accept the emotions that are in play.

✓ **Speak about yourself not about them** – use direct 'I' statements. 'Own' the problem and how it affects you.

✓ **Make your proposals consistent with other people's values** – recognise where other people are coming from. It is almost impossible to convert someone to your way of thinking unless they see the 'WIIFM' (What's In It For Me) factor. If they see a solution which fits with their world, then resolution will be easier.

✓ **Focus on interests not positions** – behind opposing positions lie shared and compatible interests, as well as conflicting ones. It's not all bad! Identify these by asking for an insight into how the other person arrived at their position. Reciprocate by sharing how you arrived at yours. Make a list of your interests and theirs; think about things from their perspective. Your understanding of what is going on may be at odds with the other person's. Be hard on the problem, not the other person.

✓ **Develop options for mutual gain** – in most disagreements and conflict situations there are three major obstacles to generating options for resolution: premature judgement; searching for a single answer, and thinking that solving someone else's problem is not your concern. To generate options, separate developing from deciding. All parties should be involved in creative exploration and design from the outset using activities such as brainstorming. Consider breaking the problem down into smaller, more manageable chunks. Look for agreements at different levels – better to have several small agreements than countless non-agreements.

The advantages of using conflict and disagreement constructively are that both can be a source of new ideas and a certain amount of each prevents an organisation, team or individual becoming complacent or lazy.

Using conflict constructively instead of destructively can help to create an organisational culture of:

- Respect for individuals.
- Active listening to, and consideration of, the views of others.
- Being open and candid with one another.
- Being supportive and helpful.
- Solving problems with total commitment.
- Mutual trust and security.

After the conflict is resolved, *evaluate the whole process*. This will help you to avoid conflict in the future and improve on the actions taken. We need to learn from our mistakes otherwise we will get drawn into the same loop time and time again. Take time to tell the rest of the team (without breaking any confidences) of any learning points.

DON'T

✗ **Hope that conflict won't occur** – the ostrich approach doesn't work!

✗ **Emphasise negative aspects of conflict** – if you tell others that you find conflict difficult, they may take advantage. As a leader you need to set an example, and as a team member you have to behave in an adult way.

✗ **Avoid conflict** – bite the bullet and deal with it.

✗ **Allow conflict to fester** – like an untreated wound it will only get worse and take longer to heal!

✗ **Personalise conflict** – it is vital that the argument does not degenerate into a slanging match. In the workplace, at least, keep it about work not any shortcomings as a person, a friend or parent.

✗ **Trivialise the other party's anger or strong emotions** – the issue may not be important to you, but accept that to the other party it might seem to be a matter of life or death.

✗ **Add to the emotional side of conflict situations** – individuals owning solutions could mean that the team becomes fragmented. There needs to be a cohesive response that strengthens the team.

8

Managing conflict 'on the spot'

> This chapter considers:
> > How to handle conflict situations 'on the
> > spot'.

Conflict situations usually happen spontaneously – no one plans them.
An individual may have taken exception to something that was said
or a look that passed. A spark is ignited and the situation becomes
volatile. One party has to defend themselves, in extreme cases,
physically. Tempers become frayed and the whole thing escalates
out of control. In a work environment, others are easily drawn into
the confrontation. As voices are raised, all those involved – whether
the original individuals or other members of the team – will begin to
take sides. Each person will have his or her own perception of what
has occurred. Sound familiar?

Cast your mind back to the conflict scenario outlined in chapter 1.
Remember, you came across two members of your team shouting at
one another in the middle of the shopfloor; a small crowd has
gathered, it looks like things might turn nasty. Hopefully, you will
now understand why the three responses suggested (going in and
shouting "What the hell's going on here, give me some answers now",
throwing a bucket of cold water over them or ignoring the situation)
are not helpful. So, what should you do? Remember, how you proceed
will not only reflect your management style but also your personal
relationship with all concerned. The organisation is relying on you to

sort conflict out at your level, and the team will be keen to see whether you are up to the job. What you choose to do next is, therefore, extremely important.

What needs to be done?

Your task as the manager is to make sense of a situation into which you have entered as quickly as possible, even though you may not know the background. You need to step in before the conflict becomes more serious, or more people are drawn into it. To this end, you need to remove those directly involved in conflict to somewhere away from the public arena (probably different areas!)

It is a good idea in the initial stages to ignore any comments that are thrown at you. They are likely to be of little value and inclined to be emotive statements based on individuals taking sides. Confrontation occurs with little thought as to outcomes. Things are said in the heat of the moment. The first casualty in any confrontation is usually the truth! Comments are made which have little basis in fact; irrational judgements are made about people. Such is the passion that can be released at this time.

Conflict needs to be seen as a breakdown in communication; a problem to be solved. It means that all those involved need to commit to sitting down and dealing with the reasons for the breakdown. The actual confrontation scene is usually only a symptom of a deeper problem. Conflict comes under the umbrella of 'behaviours'; we can therefore change how we interact with one other. This needs to be the starting point in dealing with it.

What is required is an adult, assertive response. You may need to raise your voice to get the attention of all concerned to begin with, but this should not be a trigger for more aggression. Once you have gained control, your next move needs to be decisive.

You need to establish the seriousness of the situation. Your first concern must be for the safety and welfare of the staff. Is anyone hurt? You have a duty under the (UK) law to ensure the safety of the whole staff. Is anyone else affected? Fortunately, in this instance, things haven't got physical.

Once you are sure of people's welfare, your next concern must be to restore the *status quo* – getting everyone back to work once the excitement is over. People may want to talk about the confrontation, such is human nature. It may be worthwhile to suggest some time out, perhaps a short tea-break. You need to be aware of some people's need to talk, whether they were active participants or passive bystanders. Others will just want to get back to work but could be covering up their real feelings and reactions. As the manager, you have a responsibility to deal with each person appropriately. In any case, a 'cooling off' period is definitely recommended.

Now you need to assess the severity of the situation. A minor incident should be dealt with quickly and with the minimum of fuss. A more serious incident, however, will have to be dealt with in a more systematic, formal manner. You will need to involve your HR department or a senior manager.

So what constitutes a minor incident (which you can handle informally) and what constitutes a serious incident (when you will need to involve HR and processes become more formal)? This, and how you should proceed next, is the topic of the next chapter.

Summary checklist

✓ Intervene in conflict before it escalates.

✓ Take control of the situation; remove those involved to a quiet, private area, get other people back to work.

✓ Assess whether it is a minor or more serious incident.

9

Investigation and resolution

This chapter covers:
> Assessing the seriousness of the conflict situation and whether you can, or should, get involved in investigation and resolution.
> Key elements in conflict resolution – consistent process; information gathering; review; decision and communication; evaluation; implementation.

Assessing the seriousness of a situation

What constitutes a minor incident? I would suggest:

- 'Words' exchanged in a heated discussion which are personal rather than business related.

- Inappropriate body language – slamming a door, rude gestures.

- Petty arguments between team members.

- Infringement of agreed ground rules.

When does it become more serious? I would suggest:

- Incidents where there is violence.

- Wilful abuse or damage to property.

- Disrespect of individuals as described in chapter 2 (discrimination, harassment and bullying).
- When team discipline and performance is affected, eg a 'work to rule'.
- Potential breaches of contract.
- Incidents which external agencies may need to be involved in, eg unions, police.

These suggestions are not exhaustive! Each workplace, each team and each manager will have their own idea as to the difference between minor and serious incidents; indeed, the difference may be defined in a policy. Knowing when to intervene informally and when to pass the situation to HR or a senior manager is crucial. Early intervention will nip potential problems in the bud but heavy-handedness will cause more problems.

If the incident is serious, you *must* involve your HR department or a senior manager immediately. If, however, the incident is less serious, you may be able to be involved in the investigation and resolution process.

Investigation and resolution

You need to investigate fully the circumstances of any conflict incident. So what do you need to do first? The following is a suggested process only. You will, with experience, find an approach which better reflects your way of working. Bear in mind, too, that each situation is different. What is important is that you develop a process which works for you, your team and the organisation, and which is consistent in its method. Whatever you do, you must remain impartial throughout any investigation. If this will be difficult for you (or those you are investigating doubt your impartiality), refer the investigation to the HR department or a senior manager.

back in the same predicament pretty quickly, but this time your team will know your inadequacies! Use the momentum of this process to make changes and enhance your reputation at the same time.

Throughout this whole process you must develop the following skills and attributes:

- **Impartiality** – you cannot have favourites. You need to treat everyone with the same level of commitment, confidence and opportunity. If you cannot guarantee this, or those you are investigating aren't satisfied, defer to the HR department or a senior manager.

- **Preparation** – there is an old saying that if you fail to plan, then you plan to fail. Time spent planning may seem like time wasted; it isn't. Your preferred management style might be more dynamic – more *doing* rather than thinking – but this is an occasion when you need to take your time.

- **Fairness** – this goes with impartiality and consistency.

- **Communication** – keep everyone informed. If you are not communicating with the team the assumption may be that you are hiding difficulties or hoping that the whole thing blows over. Be up-front with the team.

So is conflict all bad? Processes, behaviour, different resolution styles – it's a lot to think about. Is there a more positive side to conflict? Most emphatically *yes*. This is the subject of the next chapter.

Summary checklist

✓ Don't ignore a conflict situation; if you do it might escalate.

✓ Assess the seriousness of the conflict – is it something you can handle or should you defer to the HR department or a senior manager?

✓ If you undertake an informal investigation, develop a consistent process.

✓ Remain impartial throughout. If you, or those you are investigating, have doubts about this, defer to the HR department or a senior manager.

10

Conflict is good for you!

This chapter considers:
> Positive aspects of conflict for the team and the individual.

If you have read this far you may think that all conflict is bad. In my Introduction, however, I commented that without conflict life would be bland and uninteresting. Try to imagine your favourite film, television soap or book without conflict. Conflict adds some spice and challenge to life.

Positive aspects of conflict for the team

- **Conflict clears the air** by getting issues into the open. Throughout this book I have emphasised the need for clear communication. When individuals are able to voice their side of an issue there is an opportunity to resolve a problem. If you, as a manager, supervisor or team leader, can encourage team members to voice their opinions *in the right place and at the right time* then conflict and disagreement will be viewed more positively. Set aside time regularly to give the team an opportunity to consider potential problems both as a team and as individuals. Ask at the end of every discussion "Can anyone see any problems that we haven't thought of?"

- **It rejuvenates** team spirit and energy levels. In teams where conflict is unresolved the 'esprit de corps' flags. The team becomes de-motivated; lethargy sets in. The successful resolution of conflict invigorates team members and gets them into a more positive frame of mind.

- **Promotes creativity** by encouraging debate. When people get together and throw around ideas better solutions are created. Brainstorming sessions can appear to be conflict based. Remember, to some people conflict is perceived as noisy, heated and in direct opposition to their way of thinking – exactly what a good brainstorming session should be like! Brainstorming is a useful tool to employ when a team's creative spirit is bogged down.

- **Reveals true feelings** by its spontaneity. If someone feels passionate enough about an issue to raise their voice and get involved in an argument then it would be counter-productive to stifle those feelings. Harness those feelings and use them in a more focused discussion. Strong emotion can be a positive driver for change.

- **Provides an opportunity to improve performance** by recognising that changes need to be made. By addressing the team's worries and concerns, and including their contribution to the resolution of a conflict situation, you can gain their commitment to the outcome.

Positive aspects of conflict for the individual

As well as benefits to the team, the following benefits accrue to the individual, whether a team leader or team member.

- **Conflict releases pent-up emotions**. Negative emotions which are held in check can contribute to higher levels of stress. By bringing these emotions to the surface we can alleviate their harmful effects. The manager who is in tune with team members, and recognises the signs of growing stress levels, can offer an opportunity to resolve the conflict.

- **Restores harmony in a relationship**. Those around us – whether work colleagues, family or friends – may not be aware of our concerns. If we are in conflict with their opinions, way of doing something, ideas or perceptions, we owe it to them to raise those issues, resolve the conflict and restore the relationship. And remember, in some relationships the best part of resolving a conflict situation is the making up afterwards!

- **Encourages individual growth** and development through exploring another person's point of view. Most of us think we know best; being in conflict allows us an opportunity to venture into another person's world. We can enrich our own lives and the lives of others by sharing our perspective. It may be painful, but as the saying goes, 'No pain, no gain'.

- **Builds self-confidence.** Each time we tackle a conflict situation we gain confidence, whether as a team leader or team member. When we deal with a difficulty effectively it makes it that much easier the next time.

- **Asserts our principles.** Others gain an insight into the importance we attach to particular issues. If we never share our thoughts on an issue other people will never know where we stand on anything. Individuals who value particular issues, and are not worried about being in conflict with others, enrich debate.

- **Improves status.** By using some of the strategies outlined in this book you will be perceived as an assertive individual, able to participate in debate in a rational, open manner. By applying a fair and consistent process you will gain the respect of those around you.

- **Encourages recognition** from senior management. People who deal with conflict effectively will get noticed by those above them. Mastering the skill of conflict management could pay off with that promotion you wanted.

Summary checklist

✓ Remember that conflict isn't all bad, for you or your team. Use the opportunities it presents, as well as dealing with the threats.

Conclusion

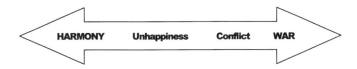

| HARMONY | Unhappiness | Conflict | WAR |

This diagram was shown in the Introduction. As we have learned, conflict is rarely as polarised as this diagram suggests.

Managers, supervisors and team leaders who communicate, at both team and individual level, and take notice of their teams, will be successful. Those who regard conflict in a positive way and deal with it accordingly will be extra successful. They are the managers who will be:

- Respected as individuals.
- Regarded as achievers.
- Able to get more from the team.
- Worth holding on to!

Team members who deal with conflict effectively will be:

- More productive.
- More confident.
- Likely to have stronger relationships with others.
- Able to handle difficulties without 'passing the buck'.
- A pleasure to work with.
- The managers of the future!

Managing conflict means:

- Recognising when it happens.
- Understanding its causes.
- Appreciating that it is a vital part of team development.
- Admitting that we have individual perceptions of what it looks like, feels like and sounds like.
- Developing an appropriate style.
- Behaving *assertively* not aggressively and encouraging the same in those around us.
- Practising the strategies suggested.
- Dealing with it, in a consistent, fair and prompt fashion.
- Keeping up to date with your own organisation's procedures.
- Developing a skill that builds self-esteem and confidence.

A final thought

The only way to improve any skill is to practise, practise, practise. Managing conflict is no different. If we ignore uncomfortable situations they don't usually improve. If we deal with conflict effectively, however, we bolster our own self-esteem and earn the respect of those around us. Senior managers and staff will gain confidence in our ability to manage. We will gain the ability to master our own destiny, whether in our personal or work life. Make the most of conflict, it's a golden opportunity to show you can manage effectively!

Bibliography

Harassment, Bullying and Violence at Work, Angela Ishmael with Bunmi Alemoru, The Industrial Society, 1999

The Fifth Discipline Fieldbook, Peter Senge, *et al*, Nicholas Brealey Publishing, 1994

Assertiveness – a Working Guide, Paddy O'Brien, Nicholas Brealey Publishing, 1992